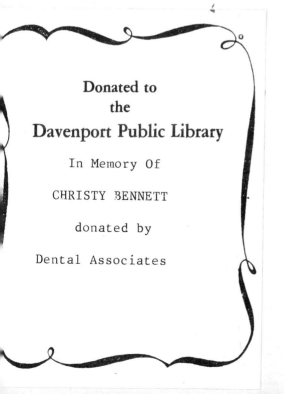

Who do you think you are?

Who do you think you are?

POEMS ABOUT PEOPLE

Chosen by David Woolger

Oxford University Press
Oxford   New York   Toronto

Oxford University Press, Walton Street, Oxford OX2 6DP

Oxford   New York   Toronto
Delhi   Bombay   Calcutta   Madras   Karachi
Petaling Jaya   Singapore   Hong Kong   Tokyo
Nairobi   Dar es Salaam   Cape Town
Melbourne   Auckland

and associated companies in
Berlin   Ibadan

Oxford is a trade mark of Oxford University Press

Selection and arrangement
© Oxford University Press 1990
First published 1990

Library of Congress Catalog Card Number: 89–043701

British Library Cataloguing in Publication Data
    Who do you think you are?
        1. Poetry in English – Anthologies
        I. Woolger, David
        821'.008

ISBN 0 19 276074 2

Typeset by Pentacor Ltd, High Wycombe, Bucks
Printed and bound in Great Britain by
Butler & Tanner Ltd, Frome and London

CONTENTS

Routines – and Doors ...

A World of Different People ...

The Peerless and the Skilled ...

Silences and Words (Sometimes, Poetry) ...

Solitudes ...

Connections ...

... and Separations ...

Nobody

I'm Nobody! Who are you?
Are you – Nobody – too?
Then there's a pair of us!
Don't tell! they'd banish us – you know!

How dreary – to be – Somebody!
How public – like a Frog –
To tell your name – the livelong June –
To an admiring Bog!

Emily Dickinson

To the memory of Aubrey Fernando

PHOSPHORUS
AND
PHANTASMAGORIA

$6 \times 5 =$

$8 \times 8 = 64$

$6 \times 3 =$

$4 \times 4 =$

Who Do You Think You Are?

Who do you think you are
and where do you think you came from?
From toenails to the hair of your head you are mixed of the
    earth, of the air,
Of compounds equal to the burning gold and amethyst lights
    of the Mountains of the Blood of Christ at Santa Fe.
Listen to the laboratory man tell you what you are made of, man,
    listen while he takes you apart.
Weighing 150 pounds you hold 3,500 cubic feet of gas – oxygen,
    hydrogen, nitrogen.
From the 22 pounds and 10 ounces of carbon in you is the filling
    for 9,000 lead pencils.
In your blood are 50 grains of iron and in the rest of your
    frame enough iron to make a spike that would hold
    your weight.
From your 50 ounces of phosphorus could be made 800,000
    matches and elsewhere in your physical premises are
    hidden 60 lumps of sugar, 20 teaspoons of salt,
    38 quarts of water, two ounces of lime, and scatterings
    of starch, chloride of potash, magnesium, sulphur,
    hydrochloric acid.
You are a walking drug store and also a cosmos and a phantasma-
    goria treading a lonesome valley, one of the people, one
    of the minions and myrmidons who would like an answer
    to the question, 'Who and what are you?'

Carl Sandburg

What Did I Dream?

What did I dream? I do not know –
    The fragments fly like chaff.
Yet, strange, my mind was tickled so
    I cannot help but laugh.

Pull the curtains close again,
    Tuck me grandly in;
Must a world of humour wane
    Because birds begin

Complaining in a fretful tone,
    Rousing me from sleep –
The finest entertainment known,
    And given rag-cheap?

Robert Graves

Dreams

My dreams are lucid.
They must be someone else's;
I'm not so clever.

Anne Bloch

To Make a Prairie

To make a prairie it takes a clover and one bee,
One clover, and a bee,
And revery.
The revery alone will do,
If bees are few.

Emily Dickinson

A Boy's Head

In it there is a space-ship
and a project
for doing away with piano lessons.

And there is
Noah's ark,
which shall be first.

And there is
an entirely new bird,
an entirely new hare,
an entirely new bumble-bee.

There is a river
that flows upwards.

There is a multiplication table.

There is anti-matter.

And it just cannot be trimmed.

I believe
that only what cannot be trimmed
is a head.

There is much promise
in the circumstance
that so many people have heads.

Miroslav Holub

Introspection

Have you ever seen a mind
thinking?
It is like an old cow
trying to get through the pub door
carrying a guitar in its mouth;
old habits keep breaking in
on the job in hand;
it keeps wanting
to do something else:
like having a bit of a graze
for example,
or galumphing round the paddock
or being a café musician
with a beret and a moustache.
But if she just keeps trying
the old cow, avec guitar,
will be through that door
as easy as pie
but she won't know how it was done.
It's harder with a piano.

Have you ever heard the havoc
of remembering?
It is like asking
the local plumber
in to explore a disused well;
down he goes on a twisting rope,
his cloddy boots
bumping against
that slimed brickwork,
and when he arrives at bottom
in the smell of darkness,
with a splash of jet black water
he grasps a huge fish,
slices it open
with his clasp-knife
and finds a gold coin inside
which slips
out of his fingers
back into the unformed unseeing,
never to be found again.

Chris Wallace-Crabbe

Mind

Mind in its purest play is like some bat
That beats about in caverns all alone,
Contriving by a kind of senseless wit
Not to conclude against a wall of stone.

It has no need to falter or explore;
Darkly it knows what obstacles are there,
And so may weave and flitter, dip and soar
In perfect courses through the blackest air.

And has this simile a like perfection?
The mind is like a bat. Precisely. Save
That in the very happiest intellection
A graceful error may correct the cave.

Richard Wilbur

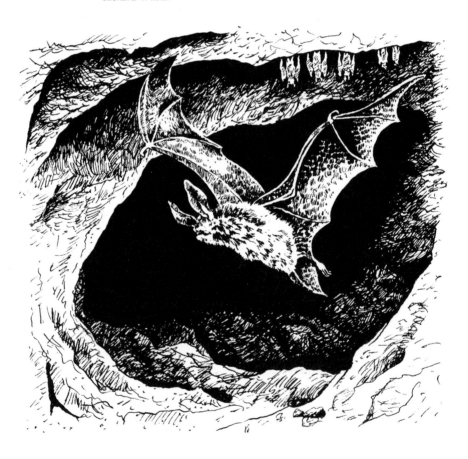

An Ordinary Day

I took my mind a walk
Or my mind took me a walk –
Whichever was the truth of it.

The light glittered on the water
Or the water glittered in the light.
Cormorants stood on a tidal rock

With their wings spread out,
Stopping no traffic. Various ducks
Shilly-shallied here and there

On the shilly-shallying water.
An occasional gull yelped. Small flowers
Were doing their level best

To bring to their kerb bees like
Aerial charabancs. Long weeds in the clear
Water did Eastern dances, unregarded

By shoals of darning needles. A cow
Started a moo but thought
Better of it ... And my feet took me home

And my mind observed to me,
Or I to it, how ordinary
Extraordinary things are or

How extraordinary ordinary
Things are, like the nature of the mind
And the process of observing.

Norman MacCaig

Healing a Lunatic Boy

Trees turned and talked to me,
Tigers sang,
Houses put on leaves,
Water rang.
Flew in, flew out
On my tongue's thread
A speech of birds
From my hurt head.

At my fine loin
Fire and cloud kissed,
Rummaged the green bone
Beneath my wrist.
I saw a sentence
Of fern and tare
Write with loud light
The mineral air.

On a stopped morning
The city spoke,
In my rich mouth
Oceans broke.
No more on the spun shore
I walked unfed.
I drank the sweet sea,
Stones were bread.

Then came the healer
Grave as grass,
His hair of water
And hands of glass.
I watched at his tongue
The white words eat,
In death, dismounted
At his stabbed feet.

Now river is river
And tree is tree,
My house stands still
As the northern sea.
On my hundred of parables
I heard him pray,
Seize my smashed world,
Wrap it away.

Now the pebble is sour,
The birds beat high,
The fern is silent,
The river dry.
A seething summer
Burned to bone
Feeds at my mouth
But finds a stone.

Charles Causley

The Human Abstract

Pity would be no more
If we did not make somebody poor;
And Mercy no more could be
If all were as happy as we.

And mutual fear brings peace,
Till the selfish loves increase:
Then Cruelty knits a snare,
And spreads his baits with care.

He sits down with holy fears,
And waters the ground with tears;
Then Humility takes its root
Underneath his foot.

Soon spreads the dismal shade
Of Mystery over his head;
And the Caterpillar and Fly
Feed on the Mystery.

And it bears the fruit of Deceit,
Ruddy and sweet to eat;
And the Raven his nest has made
In its thickest shade.

The Gods of the earth and sea
Sought thro' Nature to find this Tree;
But their search was all in vain:
There grows one in the Human Brain.

William Blake

FEELING BAD –
THEN FEELING
GOOD . . .

O! Why Was I Born with a Different Face?

O! why was I born with a different face?
Why was I not born like the rest of my race?
When I look, each one starts; when I speak, I offend;
Then I'm silent and passive, and lose every friend.

William Blake

But No One Cares

The day was long.
The winds blew on
But no one cared.

All alone,
Had no home,
But no one cared.

He fought against the wind and rain
Although he had a lot of pain,
But no one cared.

The day grew old
The night was cold
But no one cared.

The stars above
Were his only love
He left no mark
But no one cared.

He had feelings
Of his piteous meanings
But no one cared.

In the still of the night
He felt unright
But no one cared.

He could have died,
Instead he cried,
But no one cared.

Anon.

Sorrow

Why does the thin grey strand
Floating up from the forgotten
Cigarette between my fingers,
Why does it trouble me?

Ah, you will understand;
When I carried my mother downstairs,
A few times only, at the beginning
Of her soft-footed malady,

I should find, for a reprimand
To my gaiety, a few long grey hairs
On the breast of my coat; and one by one
I watched them float up the dark chimney.

D H Lawrence

Anger Lay by Me All Night Long

Anger lay by me all night long,
    His breath was hot upon my brow,
He told me of my burning wrong,
    All night he talked and would not go.

He stood by me all through the day,
    Struck from my hand the book, the pen;
He said: 'Hear first what I've to say,
    And sing, if you've the heart to, then.'

And can I cast him from my couch?
    And can I lock him from my room?
Ah no, his honest words are such
    That he's my true-lord, and my doom.

Elizabeth Daryush

Ancient Music

Winter is icummen in,
Lhude sing Goddamm,
Raineth drop and staineth slop,
And how the wind does ramm!
    Sing: Goddamm.
Skiddeth bus and sloppeth us,
An ague hath my ham.
Freezeth river, turneth liver,
    Damn you, sing: Goddamm.
Goddamm, Goddamm, 'tis why I am, Goddamm,
    So 'gainst the winter's balm.
Sing Goddamm, damm, sing Goddamm,
Sing Goddamm, sing Goddamm, DAMM.

Ezra Pound

Dust of Snow

The way a crow
Shook down on me
The dust of snow
From a hemlock tree

Has given my heart
A change of mood
And saved some part
Of a day I had rued.

Robert Frost

Dog in the Street

dog in the street
stretching
in a nice long yawn –
pure envy
I do likewise

Ishikawa Takuboku

Young Shepherd Bathing his Feet

Only the short, broad, splayed feet
Moved...

Feet that had trodden over
Soft soil,
Sand,
Ploughed veld,
Mountain rocks
And along narrow tracks,
On Winter clay and
Dust of Summer roads...

The short, broad, splayed feet
Moved
In and out...

The stumpy toes stretched wide
Apart
And closed together
Then opened again...

In ecstasy.

Peter Clarke

Two Girls Singing

It neither was the words nor yet the tune.
Any tune would have done and any words.
Any listener or no listener at all.

As nightingales in rocks or a child crooning
in its own world of strange awakening
or larks for no reason but themselves.

So on the bus through late November running
by yellow lights tormented, darkness falling,
the two girls sang for miles and miles together

and it wasn't the words or tune. It was the singing.
It was the human sweetness in that yellow,
the unpredicted voices of our kind.

Iain Crichton Smith

To a Poor Old Woman

munching a plum on
the street a paper bag
of them in her hand

They taste good to her
They taste good
to her. They taste
good to her

You can see it by
the way she gives herself
to the one half
sucked out in her hand

Comforted
a solace of ripe plums
seeming to fill the air
They taste good to her

William Carlos Williams

On Making Tea

The water bubbles
Should become happy;
Not angry.

The tea leaves
Should become excited;
But not violently so.

The pouring of the water
On the leaves
Should be a conception;
Not a confusion.

The union of the tea and water
Should be allowed to dream;
But not to sleep.

Now follow some moments of rest.

The tea is then gently poured
Into simple, clean containers,
And served before smiling
And understanding friends.

R L Wilson

Footnotes on Happiness

Happiness filters
Out through a crack in the door, through the net's reticulations.
But also in.

The old cat Patience
Watching the hole with folded paws and quiet tail
Can seldom catch it.

Time tables fail.
It rarely stands at a certain moment a certain day
At a certain bus-stop.

You cannot say
It will keep an appointment, or pass the same street corner twice.
Nor say it won't.

Lavender, ice,
Camphor, glass cases, vacuum chambers hermetically sealed,
Won't keep it fresh.

It will not yield
Except to the light, the careless, the accidental hand,
And easily bruises.

It is brittle as sand.
It is more and less than you hoped to find. It has never quite
Your own ideas.

It shows no spite
Or favour in choosing its host. It is, like God,
Casual, odd

A S J Tessimond

YOUNG
AND
OLD . . .

Children's Song

We live in our own world,
A world that is too small
For you to stoop and enter
Even on hands and knees,
The adult subterfuge.
And though you probe and pry
With analytic eye,
And eavesdrop all our talk
With an amused look,
You cannot find the centre
Where we dance, where we play,
Where life is still asleep
Under the closed flower,
Under the smooth shell
Of eggs in the cupped nest
That mock the faded blue
of your remoter heaven.

R S Thomas

Let Me Die a Youngman's Death

Let me die a youngman's death
not a clean & inbetween
the sheets holywater death
not a famous-last-words
peaceful out of breath death

When I'm 73
& in constant good tumour
may I be mown down at dawn
by a bright red sports car
on my way home
from an allnight party

Or when I'm 91
with silver hair
& sitting in a barber's chair
may rival gangsters
with hamfisted tommyguns burst in
& give me a short back & insides

Or when I'm 104
& banned from the Cavern
may my mistress
catching me in bed with her daughter
& fearing her son
cut me up into little pieces
& throw away every piece but one

Let me die a youngman's death
not a free from sin tiptoe in
candle wax and waning death
not a curtains drawn by angels borne
'what a nice way to go' death

Roger McGough

Child or Adult?

Am I a child or an adult?
No! Not a child now – my dolls are gone;
My dream world has rippled away.
I am tall, I understand adult talk,
But does that mean that I am an adult?

Am I an adult or a child?
No! Not an adult – I couldn't look after myself;
The understanding is just not there.
I pay a half fare on a bus to school,
But does that mean that I am a child?

Am I a child or an adult?
No! Not a child now – it's not a teddy I love;
His cherished position is taken.
Just because my toys have lost their value,
Does that mean that I am an adult?

Am I an adult or a child?
No! Not an adult – I do not see
The reasons for adult disputes;
I am safe in non-understanding,
But does that mean that I am a child?

Well, am I a child or an adult?
No! Not one or the other now;
One pace in front of childhood,
And one behind an adult.
Soon I shall stride into a new world,
The world of adult life.

Margaret Lawrence

Childhood

I used to think that grown-up people chose
To have stiff backs and wrinkles round their nose,
And veins like small fat snakes on either hand,
On purpose to be grand.
Till through the banisters I watched one day
My great-aunt Etty's friend who was going away,
And how her onyx beads had come unstrung.
I saw her grope to find them as they rolled;
And then I knew that she was helplessly old,
As I was helplessly young.

Frances Cornford

Follower

My father worked with a horse-plough,
His shoulders globed like a full sail strung
Between the shafts and the furrow.
The horses strained at his clicking tongue.

An expert. He would set the wing
And fit the bright steel-pointed sock.
The sod rolled over without breaking.
At the headrig, with a single pluck

Of reins, the sweating team turned round
And back into the land. His eye
Narrowed and angled at the ground,
Mapping the furrow exactly.

I stumbled in his hob-nailed wake,
Fell sometimes on the polished sod;
Sometimes he rode me on his back
Dipping and rising to his plod.

I wanted to grow up and plough,
To close one eye, stiffen my arm.
All I ever did was follow
In his broad shadow round the farm.

I was a nuisance, tripping, falling,
Yapping always. But today
It is my father who keeps stumbling
Behind me, and will not go away.

Seamus Heaney

Grandmother and Child

The waves that danced about the rock have gone,
The tide has stolen the rock as time has stolen
The quiet old lady who waited beneath the trees
That moved with a sad sea-sound in the summer wind.

When death was as near as the wind among the leaves,
Troubling the waking fear in the heart of the child
As the wind was troubling the shadows on the sunlit lawn,
The grandmother seemed as frail as the frailest leaf.

But she sat so still in the shade of the summer trees
With the wind of death on her cheeks and her folded hands,
Her strength seemed large and cool, as the rock in the sea
Seemed large and cool in the green and restless waves.

As the rock remains in the sea, deep down and strong,
The rock-like strength of the lady beneath the tree
Remains in the mind of the child, more real than death,
To challenge the child's strength in the hour of fear.

Ruth Dallas

Ninetieth Birthday

You go up the long track
That will take a car, but is best walked
On slow feet, noting the lichen
That writes history on the page
Of the grey rock. Trees are about you
At first, but yield to the green bracken,
The nightjar's house: you can hear it spin
On warm evenings; it is still now
In the noonday heat, only the lesser
Voices sound, blue-fly and gnat
And the stream's whisper. As the road climbs,
You will pause for breath and the far sea's
Signal will flash, till you turn again
To the steep track, buttressed with cloud.

And there at the top that old woman,
Born almost a century back
In that stone farm, awaits your coming;
Waits for the news of the lost village
She thinks she knows, a place that exists
In her memory only.

                        You bring her greeting
And praise for having lasted so long
With time's knife shaving the bone.
Yet no bridge joins her own
World with yours, all you can do
Is lean kindly across the abyss
To hear words that were once wise.

R S Thomas

How to Be Old

It is easy to be young. (Everybody is,
at first.) It is not easy
to be old. It takes time.
Youth is given; age is achieved.
One must work a magic to mix with time
in order to become old.

Youth is given. One must put it away
like a doll in a closet,
take it out and play with it only
on holidays. One must have many dresses
and dress the doll impeccably
(but not to show the doll, to keep it hidden.)

It is necessary to adore the doll,
to remember it in the dark on the ordinary
days, and every day congratulate
one's ageing face in the mirror.

In time one will be very old.
In time, one's life will be accomplished.
And in time, in time, the doll –
like new, though ancient – will be found.

May Swenson

ROUTINES – AND DOORS . . .

Time and Motion Study

Slow down the film. You see that bit.
Seven days old and no work done.
Two hands clutching nothing but air,
Two legs kicking nothing but air.
That yell. That's wasted energy there.
No use to himself, no good for the firm.
Make a note of that.

New film. Now look, now he's fourteen.
Work out the energy required
To make him grow that tall.
It could have been used
It could have all been used
For the good of the firm and he could have stayed small.
Make a note of that.

Age thirty. And the waste continues.
Using his legs for walking. Tiring
His mouth with talking and eating. Twitching.
Slow it down. Reproducing? I see.
All, I suppose, for the good of the firm.
But he'd better change methods. Yes, he'd better.
Look at the waste of time and emotion.
Look at the waste. Look. Look.
And make a note of that.

Adrian Mitchell

The Unknown Citizen

(To JS/07/M/378
This Marble Monument
Is Erected by the State)

He was found by the Bureau of Statistics to be
One against whom there was no official complaint,
And all the reports on his conduct agree
That, in the modern sense of an old-fashioned word, he was a saint,
For in everything he did he served the Greater Community.
Except for the War till the day he retired
He worked in a factory and never got fired,
But satisfied his employers, Fudge Motors Inc.
Yet he wasn't a scab or odd in his views,
For his Union reports that he paid his dues,
(Our report on his Union shows it was sound)
And our Social Psychology workers found
That he was popular with his mates and liked a drink.
The Press are convinced that he bought a paper every day
And that his reactions to advertisements were normal in every way.
Policies taken out in his name prove that he was fully insured,
And his Health-card shows he was once in hospital but left it cured.
Both Producers Research and High-Grade Living declare
He was fully sensible to the advantages of the Instalment Plan
And had everything necessary to the Modern Man,
A phonograph, a radio, a car and a frigidaire.
Our researchers into Public Opinion are content
That he held the proper opinions for the time of year;
When there was peace, he was for peace; when there was war, he went.
He was married and added five children to the population,
Which our Eugenist says was the right number for a parent of his
    generation,
And our teachers report that he never interfered with their education.
Was he free? Was he happy? The question is absurd:
Had anything been wrong, we should certainly have heard.

W H Auden

The Legs

There was this road,
And it led up-hill,
And it led down-hill,
And round and in and out.

And the traffic was legs,
Legs from the knees down,
Coming and going,
Never pausing.

And the gutters gurgled
With the rain's overflow,
And the sticks on the pavement
Blindly tapped and tapped.

What drew the legs along
Was the never-stopping,
And the senseless, frightening
Fate of being legs.

Legs for the road,
The road for legs,
Resolutely nowhere
In both directions.

My legs at least
Were not in that rout:
On grass by the road-side
Entire I stood,

Watching the unstoppable
Legs go by
With never a stumble
Between step and step.

Though my smile was broad
The legs could not see,
Though my laugh was loud
The legs could not hear.

My head dizzied, then:
I wondered suddenly,
Might I too be a walker
From the knees down?

Gently I touched my shins.
The doubt unchained them:
They had run in twenty puddles
Before I regained them.

Robert Graves

Ambition

I got pocketed behind 7X–3824;
He was making 65, but I can do a little more.
I crowded him on the curves, but I couldn't get past,
And on the straightways there was always some truck coming fast.
Then we got to the top of a mile-long incline
And I edged her out to the left, a little over the white line,
And ahead was a long grade with construction at the bottom,
And I said to the wife, 'Now by golly I got'm!'
I bet I did 85 going down the long grade,
And I braked her down hard in front of the barricade,
And I swung in ahead of him and landed fine
Behind 9W–7679.

Morris Bishop

Toads

Why should I let the toad *work*
    Squat on my life?
Can't I use my wit as a pitchfork
    And drive the brute off?

Six days of the week it soils
    With its sickening poison –
Just for paying a few bills!
    That's out of proportion.

Lots of folk live on their wits:
    Lecturers, lispers,
Losels, loblolly-men, louts –
    They don't end as paupers;

Lots of folk live up lanes
    With fires in a bucket,
Eat windfalls and tinned sardines –
    They seem to like it.

Their nippers have got bare feet,
    Their unspeakable wives
Are skinny as whippets – and yet
    No one actually *starves*.

Ah, were I courageous enough
    To shout *Stuff your pension!*
But I know, all too well, that's the stuff
    That dreams are made on:

For something sufficiently toad-like
    Squats in me, too;
Its hunkers are heavy as hard luck,
    And cold as snow,

And will never allow me to blarney
    My way to getting
The fame and the girl and the money
    All at one sitting.

I don't say, one bodies the other
    One's spiritual truth;
But I do say it's hard to lose either,
    When you have both.

Philip Larkin

Work is Love

Work is love made visible.
And if you cannot work with love
But only with distaste, it is better
That you should leave your work and
Sit at the gate of the temple and take
Alms from those who work with joy.

Anon.

Living off Other People – Welfare

It would be pretty to have roses
Flourishing by my back door.
It would be nice to have a well-kept house
With velvet chairs not scraping a polished floor.
It would be lovely to sit down at dinner
Grey tie, pearl pin, fresh shirt and well-kept hands
And good to have a purring car in a clean garage
Eye-catching as the best brass bands.

But to keep it all going would be a lot of worry
And anyone who does it has to race and scurry
Seeing to roofs and pruning, maintenance and mechanics,
A shower of rain, a little greenfly, bring on terrible panics
And ruin and failure shadow every path.

So I think this is the best thing to do:
As I walk down roads I see so many flowers
Nod-nodding in all the gardens that I pass.
I can glance into other people's rooms that they have furnished
And look how courteously that man is turning
To open the front door to his gleaming house.
Did you see how his suit fitted him, his perfect cuffs? Spotless cars
Slide by with women in furs and perfumes
Wafted to me with the flavour of cigars.

I am wrapped in my layers of shapeless coats
And I need never polish or dig or set
The table out for four distinguished guests
Or get to an office or prove myself each day
To provide for hammocks and lawns.
To get my antiques protected against insects.
A guest everywhere, I look in as dinner is served.
As I tramp past others' gardens, the rose opens.

Jenny Joseph

The Door

Go and open the door.
  Maybe outside there's
  a tree, or a wood,
  a garden,
  or a magic city.

Go and open the door.
  Maybe a dog's rummaging.
  Maybe you'll see a face,
or an eye,
or the picture
        of a picture.

Go and open the door.
  If there's a fog
  it will clear.

Go and open the door.
  Even if there's only
  the darkness ticking,
  even if there's only
  the hollow wind,
  even if
      nothing
        is there,
go and open the door.

At least
there'll be
a draught.

Miroslav Holub

may my heart always

may my heart always be open to little
birds who are the secrets of living
whatever they sing is better than to know
and if men should not hear them men are old

may my mind stroll about hungry
and fearless and thirsty and supple
and even if it's sunday may i be wrong
for whenever men are right they are not young

and may myself do nothing usefully
and love yourself so more than truly
there's never been quite such a fool who could fail
pulling all the sky over him with one smile

e e cummings

A WORLD OF DIFFERENT PEOPLE . . .

Street Boy

Just you look at me, man,
Stompin' down the street
My crombie's stuffed with biceps
My boots is filled with feet.

Just you hark to me, man,
When they call us out
My head is full of silence
My mouth is full of shout.

Just you watch me move, man,
Steady like a clock
My heart is spaced on blue beat
My soul is toned on rock.

Just you read my name, man,
Writ for all to see
The walls is red with stories
The streets is filled with me.

Gareth Owen

Timothy Winters

Timothy Winters comes to school
With eyes as wide as a football-pool,
Ears like bombs and teeth like splinters:
A blitz of a boy is Timothy Winters.

His belly is white, his neck is dark,
And his hair is an exclamation-mark.
His clothes are enough to scare a crow
And through his britches the blue winds blow.

When teacher talks he won't hear a word
And he shoots down dead the arithmetic-bird,
He licks the patterns off his plate
And he's not even heard of the Welfare State.

Timothy Winters has bloody feet
And he lives in a house on Suez Street,
He sleeps in a sack on the kitchen floor
And they say there aren't boys like him any more.

Old Man Winters likes his beer
And his missus ran off with a bombardier,
Grandma sits in the grate with a gin
And Timothy's dosed with an aspirin.

The Welfare Worker lies awake
But the law's as tricky as a ten-foot snake,
So Timothy Winters drinks his cup
And slowly goes on growing up.

At Morning Prayers the Master helves
For children less fortunate than ourselves,
And the loudest response in the room is when
Timothy Winters roars 'Amen!'

So come one angel, come on ten:
Timothy Winters says 'Amen
Amen amen amen amen.'
Timothy Winters, Lord.
                    Amen.

Charles Causley

Miniver Cheevy

Miniver Cheevy, child of scorn,
   Grew lean while he assailed the seasons;
He wept that he was ever born,
   And he had reasons.

Miniver loved the days of old
   When swords were bright and steeds were prancing;
The vision of a warrior bold
   Would set him dancing.

Miniver sighed for what was not,
   And dreamed, and rested from his labors;
He dreamed of Thebes and Camelot,
   And Priam's neighbors.

Miniver mourned the ripe renown
   That made so many a name so fragrant;
He mourned Romance, now on the town,
   And Art, a vagrant.

Miniver loved the Medici,
   Albeit he had never seen one;
He would have sinned incessantly
   Could he have been one.

Miniver cursed the commonplace
   And eyed a khaki suit with loathing;
He missed the medieval grace
   Of iron clothing.

Miniver scorned the gold he sought,
   But sore annoyed was he without it;
Miniver thought, and thought, and thought,
   And thought about it.

Miniver Cheevy, born too late,
   Scratched his head and kept on thinking;
Miniver coughed, and called it fate,
   And kept on drinking.

Edwin Arlington Robinson

A Polished Performance

Citizens of the polished capital
   Sigh for the towns up country,
And their innocent simplicity.

People in the towns up country
   Applaud the unpolished innocence
Of the distant villages.

Dwellers in the distant villages
   Speak of a simple unspoilt girl,
Living alone, deep in the bush.

Deep in the bush we found her,
   Large and innocent of eye,
Among gentle gibbons and mountain ferns.

Perfect for the part, perfect,
   Except for the dropsy
Which comes from polished rice.

In the capital our film is much admired,
   Its gentle gibbons and mountain ferns,
Unspoilt, unpolished, large and innocent of eye.

D J Enright

John Arthur

John Arthur walks the tideline-scribbled sand,
having nothing else to do but let things slide,
driftwood, wreckage, weed kicked into mounds,
poked and prodded, taffled and let bide.

You'd think, his tar-smeared rain-stained mac
flapping at every slouched lunge of the knee,
he had a wisdom that we strangers lack,
some slow-tongued gnomon of sand, wind, and sea,

and was content. You'd think that, if you could,
unwilling to believe him derelict,
walking beside great waters whose brown flood
roars down a wreckers' harvest to be picked –

kindling (of course) its staple, but much more
washed from the fat black coasters as they roll –
you'd figure him an uncrowned ignorant Lear
trapped on the blustered edges of the world,

and you'd be wrong all through, because John Arthur
has nothing else to do but let things slide;
driftwood and sunlight, weed and wanting, slither
endlessly through him like the sour brown tide,

and days are just for filling in with time.
Get closer and you'll see his sandblind stare.
One foot drags, one hand twitches, waves crash down
and mile and mile on mile destroy the shore.

Robin Skelton

Tramp

A knock at the door
And he stands there,
A tramp with his can
Asking for tea,
Strong for a poor man
On his way – where?

He looks at his feet,
I look at the sky;
Over us the planes build
The shifting rafters
Of that new world
We have sworn by.

I sleep in my bed,
He sleeps in the old,
Dead leaves of a ditch.
My dreams are haunted;
Are his dreams rich?
If I wake early,
He wakes cold.

R S Thomas

53

The Gardener

He was not able to read or write,
He did odd jobs on gentlemen's places
Cutting the hedge or hoeing the drive
With the smile of a saint,
With the pride of a feudal chief,
For he was not quite all there.

Crippled by rheumatism
By the time his hair was white,
He would reach the garden by twelve,
His legs in soiled puttees,
A clay pipe in his teeth,
A tiny flag in his cap,
A white cat behind him,
And his eyes a cornflower blue.

And between the clack of his shears
Or the honing of the scythe
Or the rattle of the rake on the gravel
He would talk to amuse the children,
He would talk to amuse himself or the cat
Or the robin waiting for worms
Perched on the handle of the spade;
Would remember snatches of verse
From the elementary school
About a bee and a wasp
Or the cat by the barndoor spinning;
And would talk about himself for ever –
You would never find his like –
Always in the third person;
And he would level his stick like a gun
(With a glint in his eye)
Saying 'Now I'm a Frenchman' –
He was not quite right in the head.

Louis MacNeice

Croft

Aloft,
In the loft,
Sits Croft;
He is soft.

Stevie Smith

Terminal

A small boy, four years
Or so of age,
And tired and confused,
In a noisy, crowded building,
His ears still hurting
From some mysterious ailment.
He trails behind his parents,
Tired too, if less confused.

Then the people all take sides,
Like in a game,
His father joins the Caucasian file,
His mother the Other.
Which team is his team?
He hears them talking,
His English father, Chinese mother,
And the man who owns the building,

Who rubs his head:
'There's this queue and there's that queue,
There isn't any third queue.
I don't know what to say!'

Neither does the little boy,
He is tired and confused.
In front of him the two queues stretch away,
There isn't any third queue.

D J Enright

Green Man, Blue Man

As I was walking through Guildhall Square
I smiled to see a green man there,
But when I saw him coming near
My heart was filled with nameless fear.

As I was walking through Madford Lane
A blue man stood there in the rain.
I asked him in by my front-door,
For I'd seen a blue man before.

As I was walking through Landlake Wood
A grey man in the forest stood,
But when he turned and said, 'Good day'
I shook my head and ran away.

As I was walking by Church Stile
A purple man spoke there a while.
I spoke to him because, you see,
A purple man once lived by me.

But when the night falls dark and fell
How, O how, am I to tell
Grey man, green man, purple, blue,
Which is which is which of you?

Charles Causley

THE PEERLESS
AND THE
SKILLED . . .

Mrs Reece Laughs

Laughter, with us, is no great undertaking,
A sudden wave that breaks and dies in breaking.
Laughter, with Mrs Reece, is much less simple:
It germinates, it spreads, dimple by dimple,
From small beginnings, things of easy girth,
To formidable redundancies of mirth.
Clusters of subterranean chuckles rise
And presently the circles of her eyes
Close into slits, and all the woman heaves
As a great elm with all its mounds of leaves
Wallows before the storm. From hidden sources
A mustering of blind volcanic forces
Takes her and shakes her till she sobs and gapes.
Then all that load of bottled mirth escapes
In one wild crow, a lifting of huge hands,
And creaking stays, and visage that expands
In scarlet ridge and furrow. Thence collapse,
A hanging head, a feeble hand that flaps
An apron-end to stir an air and waft
A steaming face. And Mrs Reece has laughed.

Martin Armstrong

Peerless Jim Driscoll

I saw Jim Driscoll fight in nineteen ten.
That takes you back a bit. You don't see men
Like Driscoll any more. The breed's died out.
There's no one fit to lace his boots about.
All right son. Have your laugh. You know it all.
You think these mugs today that cuff and maul
Their way through ten or fifteen threes can fight:
They hardly know their left hand from their right.
But Jim, he knew: he never slapped or swung,
His left hand flickered like a cobra's tongue
And when he followed with the old one-two
Black lightning of those fists would dazzle you.
By Jesus he could hit. I've never seen
A sweeter puncher: every blow as clean
As silver. *Peerless Jim* the papers named him,
And yet he never swaggered, never bragged.
I saw him once when he got properly tagged –
A sucker punch from nowhere on the chin –
And he was hurt; but all he did was grin
And nod as if to say, 'I asked for that.'
No one was ever more worth looking at;
Up there beneath the ache of arc-lamps he
Was just like what we'd love our sons to be
Or like those gods you've heard about at school ...
Well, yes, I'm old; and maybe I'm a fool.
I only saw him once outside the ring
And I admit I found it disappointing.
He looked just – I don't know – just ordinary,
And smaller, too, than what I thought he'd be:
An ordinary man in fact, like you or me.

Vernon Scannell

George and the Dragonfly

Georgie Jennings was spit almighty.
When the golly was good
he could down a dragonfly at 30 feet
and drown a 100 midges with the fallout.
At the drop of a cap
he would outspit lads
years older and twice his size.
Freckled and rather frail
he assumed the quiet dignity
beloved of schoolboy heroes.

But though a legend in his own playtime
Georgie Jennings failed miserably in the classroom
and left school at 15 to work for his father.
And talents such as spitting
are considered unbefitting
for upandcoming porkbutchers.

I haven't seen him since,
but like to imagine some summer soirée
when, after a day moistening mince,
George and his wife entertain tanned friends.
And after dinner, sherrytongued talk
drifts back to schooldays
the faces halfrecalled, the adventures
overexaggerated. And the next thing
that shy sharpshooter of days gone by
is led, vainly protesting, on to the lawn,
where, in the hush of a golden August evening
a reputation, 20 years tall, is put to the test.
So he takes extra care as yesterheroes must,
fires, and a dragonfly, incapsulated, bites the dust.
Then amidst bravos and tinkled applause,
blushing, Georgie leads them back indoors.

Roger McGough

The Diviner

Cut from the green hedge a forked hazel stick
That he held tight by the arms of the V:
Circling the terrain, hunting the pluck
Of water, nervous, but professionally

Unfussed. The pluck came sharp as a sting.
The rod jerked down with precise convulsions,
Spring water suddenly broadcasting
Through a green aerial its secret stations.

The bystanders would ask to have a try.
He handed them the rod without a word.
It lay dead in their grasp till nonchalantly
He gripped expectant wrists. The hazel stirred.

Seamus Heaney

How to Catch Tiddlers

(for Stephen)

Watch the net drift. Grey tides
Mingle what purposes your eye supposed
But watch the net. There is no fish
Only the net, the way it moves. There is no fish,
Forget the fish. The net is spread
And moving. Steer gently. Keep the hand
Pressured constantly against the stream.
There is no catch now, only the net
And your pressure and your poise. Below,
Ignore the pebbles and the promising weed
Mooning over its secrets. There is just the net,
The hand, and, now, near an old glance somewhere
A sleek shape holding its body constant,
Firm in its fluid world. Move on. Watch
Only the net. You are a hand only,
Steering, controlling. Now look.
Inside that silent bulge the shape
Breaks black and firm. You may rise,
You may rise now – the deftest
Turn of wrist will do it. Your hand
Crude again can support the cling of mesh.
You can relax, coldly note
The titchy black squirm. You have achieved.
Commit success to jam jars. Lean again.
Dip the slack net. Let it belly.

Brian Jones

The Watch

When I
took my
watch to the watchfixer I
felt privileged but also pained to watch the operation. He
had long fingernails and a voluntary squint. He
fixed a magnifying cup over his
squint eye. He
undressed my
watch. I
watched him
split her
in three layers and lay her
middle – a quivering viscera – in a circle on a little plinth. He
shoved shirtsleeves up and leaned like an ogre over my
naked watch. With critical pincers he
poked and stirred. He
lifted out little private things with a magnet too tiny for me
to watch almost. 'Watch out!' I
almost said. His
eye watched, enlarged, the secrets of my
watch, and I
watched anxiously. Because what if he
touched her
ticker too rough, and she
gave up the ghost out of pure fright? Or put her
things back backwards so she'd
run backwards after this? Or he
might lose a minuscule part, connected to her
exquisite heart, and mix her
up, instead of fix her.
And all the time,
all the time-
pieces on the walls, on the shelves, told the time,
told the time
in swishes and ticks,
swishes and ticks,
and seemed to be gloating, as they watched and told. I
felt faint, I
was about to lose my

breath – my
ticker going lickety-split – when watchfixer clipped her
three slices together with a gleam and two flicks of his
tools like chopsticks. He
spat out his
eye, lifted her
high, gave her
a twist, set her
hands right, laid her
little face, quite as usual, in its place on my
wrist.

May Swenson

SILENCES
AND WORDS
(SOMETIMES, POETRY) . . .

Silence

Silence: one would willingly
Consume it, eat it like bread.
There is never enough. Now,
When we are silent, metal
Still rings upon shuddering
Metal; a door slams; a child
Cries; other lives around us.

But remember, there is no
Silence within; the belly
Sighs, grumbles, and what is that
Loud knocking, that summoning?
A drum beats, a drum beats. Hear
Your own noisy machine, which
Is moving towards silence.

Edward Lucie-Smith

Silent, But ...

I may be silent, but
I'm thinking.
I may not talk, but
Don't mistake me for a wall.

Tsuboi Shigeji

Teevee

In the house
of Mr and Mrs Spouse
he and she
would watch teevee
and never a word
between them spoken
until the day
the set was broken.

Then 'How do you do?'
said he to she,
'I don't believe
that we've met yet.
Spouse is my name.
What's yours?' he asked.

'Why, mine's the same!'
said she to he,
'Do you suppose that we could be – ?'

But the set came suddenly right about,
and so they never did find out.

Eve Merriam

Just a Word

When dogs encounter
They hesitate,
They sense a kinship
Stop, sniff, then part.

As birds glide they tune
A mutual note,
Beak to beak greetings flare
To form the music of the air.

Even cups in a tray
Make a sound as they touch;
Leaves rustle;
Yet the human voice is hushed.

Strangers silently we passed
Only to look behind:
The other's head has also turned
As if to greet my mind.

Sheikha A El-Miskery

Frogs

The storm broke, and it rained,
And water rose in the pool,
And frogs hopped into the gutter,

With their skins of yellow and green,
And just their eyes shining above the surface
Of the warm solution of slime.

At night, when fireflies trace
Light-lines between the trees and flowers
Exhaling perfume,

The frogs speak to each other
In rhythm. The sound is monstrous,
But their voices are filled with satisfaction.

In the city I pine for the country;
In the country I long for conversation –
Our happy croaking.

Louis Simpson

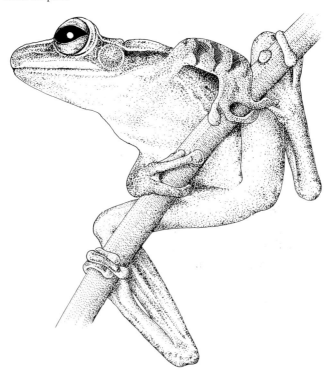

Talk

I wish people, when you sit near them,
wouldn't think it necessary to make conversation
and send thin draughts of words
blowing down your neck and your ears
and giving you a cold in your inside.

D H Lawrence

The Traveller's Curse after Misdirection

(From the Welsh)

May they wander stage by stage
Of the same vain pilgrimage,
Stumbling on, age after age,
Night and day, mile after mile,
At each and every step, a stile;
At each and every stile, withal,
May they catch their feet and fall;
At each and every fall they take,
May a bone within them break,
And may the bones that break within
Not be, for variation's sake,
Now rib, now thigh, now arm, now shin,
But always, without fail, THE NECK.

Robert Graves

Blue Umbrellas

'The thing that makes a blue umbrella with its tail –
How do you call it?' you ask. Poorly and pale
Comes my answer. For all I can call it is peacock.

Now that you go to school, you will learn how we call all sorts
    of things;
How we mar great works by our mean recital.
You will learn, for instance, that Head Monster is not the
    gentleman's accepted title;
The blue-tailed eccentrics will be merely peacocks; the dead
    bird will no longer doze
Off till tomorrow's lark, for the letter has killed him.
The dictionary is opening, the gay umbrellas close.

    Oh our mistaken teachers! –
It is not a proper respect for words that we need,
But a decent regard for things, those older creatures and more
    real.
Later you may even resort to writing verse
To prove the dishonesty of names and their black greed –
To confess your ignorance, to expiate your crime, seeking one
    spell to lift another curse.
Or you may, more commodiously, spy on your children, busy
    discoverers,
Without the dubious benefit of rhyme.

D J Enright

Words and Monsters

When he was eight years old he had become
Hungry for words, and he would munch his way
Through comics, adverts, anything with some
Printed food to hold the pangs at bay.
His friends would hoard up birds' eggs, shells or stamps,
But he collected words. One day he saw –
As he walked lonely down the town's main street –
A poster done in thunderous colours, raw
And red as flesh of newly butchered meat:
A picture of a lady, mouth distressed,
Eyes wild and fat with fear; and, underneath,
These glaring words: THE ABYSMAL BRUTE – *The Best
Movie of the Year*. He felt his teeth
Bite on the word *abysmal* as you test
The goodness of a coin. This one was fine.
He took it home to add it to the rest
Of his collection. He liked its shape and shine
But did not know its worth. Inside his head
Its echo rang. He asked his mother what
Abysmal meant. 'Bottomless,' she said.

The Abysmal Brute was grunting in the hot
Dark outside, would follow him to bed.

Vernon Scannell

Some Opposites

What is the opposite of *riot?*
It's *lots of people keeping quiet.*

The opposite of *doughnut?* Wait
A minute while I meditate.
This isn't easy. Ah, I've found it!
A cookie with a hole around it.

What is the opposite of *two?*
A lonely me, a lonely you.

The opposite of a *cloud* could be
A white reflection in the sea,
Or *a huge blueness in the air,*
Caused by a cloud's not being there.

The opposite of *opposite?*
That's much too difficult. I quit.

Richard Wilbur

Primer Lesson

Look out how you use proud words.
When you let proud words go, it is not easy to call them back.
They wear long boots, hard boots; they walk off proud; they can't hear you
     calling –
Look out how you use proud words.

Carl Sandburg

Crickets

One cricket said to another –
come, let us be ridiculous, and say love!
love love love love love
let us be absurd, woman, and say hate!
hate hate hate hate hate
and then let us be angelic and say nothing.

And the other cricket said to the first –
fool! fool! speak! speak! speak!
speak if you must, but speaking, speaking, speaking
what does it get us, what does it get us, what?
giving is love, giving is love, give!

One cricket said to another –
what is love what is love what is love
act – speak – act – speak – act – speak
give – take – give – take – give – take
more slowly as the autumn comes, but giving
and taking still, – you taking and I giving!

And the other cricket said to the first –
yes! yes! yes! you give your word!
words words but what at the end are words
speech speech what is the use of speech
give me love give me love
love!

One cricket said to another –
in the beginning – I forget – in the beginning –
fool fool fool fool fool
too late to remember and too late to teach –
in the beginning was the word, the speech,
and in the end the word, the word, the word ...

But while they quarrelled, these two foolish crickets,
and bandied act with word, denying each,
weighing their actions out in terms of speech,
the frost came whitely down and furred them both,
the speech grew slower, and the action nil,
and, at the end, even the word was still;
and god began again.

Conrad Aiken

Expression of Feelings

Only be willing to search for poetry, and there will be poetry:
My soul, a tiny speck, is my tutor.
Evening sun and fragrant grass are common things,
But, with understanding, they can become glorious verse.

Mei Yüan

Even in a Little Thing

Even in a little thing
(A leaf, a child's hand, a star's flicker)
I shall find a song worth singing
If my eyes are wide, and sleep not.

Even in a laughable thing
(Oh, hark! The children are laughing!)
There is that which fills the heart to overflowing,
And makes dream wistful.

Small is the life of man
(Not too sad, not too happy):
I shall find my songs in a man's small life. Behold them soaring!
Very low on earth are the frigate-birds hatched,
Yet they soar as high as the sun.

Anon. (trad. Micronesia)

Write a Poem

'Write a poem,' our teacher said
'A poem about an animal or a place,
Something that happened to you
In the holidays.
Better still write about yourself.
What you feel like
What's inside you
And wants to come out'.
Stephen straightaway
Began to write slowly
And went on and on
Without looking up.
John sighed and looked far away
Then suddenly snatched up his pen
And was scribbling and scribbling.
Ann tossed back her long hair
And smiled as she began.
But I sat still.
I thought of fighting cats
With chewed ears
And dogs sniffing their way along
Windy streets strewn with paper
But there seemed nothing new
To say about them ...
The holidays? Nothing much happened.
And what's inside me?
Only the numbness of cold fingers.
The grey of the sky today.
John sighed again.
Peter coughed.
Papers rustled.
Pens scratched.
A blowfly was fuzzing
At a window pane.
The tittering clock
Kept snatching the minutes away
I had nothing to say.

Olive Dove

The Thought-Fox

I imagine this midnight moment's forest:
Something else is alive
Beside the clock's loneliness
And this blank page where my fingers move.

Through the window I see no star:
Something more near
Though deeper within darkness
Is entering the loneliness:

Cold, delicately as the dark snow,
A fox's nose touches twig, leaf;
Two eyes serve a movement, that now
And again now, and now, and now

Sets neat prints into the snow
Between trees, and warily a lame
Shadow lags by stump and in hollow
Of a body that is bold to come

Across clearings, an eye,
A widening deepening greenness,
Brilliantly, concentratedly,
Coming about its own business

Till, with a sudden sharp hot stink of fox
It enters the dark hole of the head.
The window is starless still; the clock ticks,
The page is printed.

Ted Hughes

SOLITUDES . . .

Mending Wall

Something there is that doesn't love a wall,
That sends the frozen-ground-swell under it,
And spills the upper boulders in the sun;
And makes gaps even two can pass abreast.
The work of hunters is another thing:
I have come after them and made repair
Where they have left not one stone on a stone,
But they would have the rabbit out of hiding,
To please the yelping dogs. The gaps I mean,
No one has seen them made or heard them made,
But at spring mending-time we find them there.
I let my neighbour know beyond the hill;
And on a day we meet to walk the line
And set the wall between us once again.
We keep the wall between us as we go.
To each the boulders that have fallen to each.
And some are loaves and some so nearly balls
We have to use a spell to make them balance:
'Stay where you are until our backs are turned!'
We wear our fingers rough with handling them.
Oh, just another kind of outdoor game,
One on a side. It comes to little more:
There where it is we do not need the wall:
He is all pine and I am apple orchard.
My apple trees will never get across
And eat the cones under his pines, I tell him.
He only says, 'Good fences make good neighbours.'
Spring is the mischief in me, and I wonder
If I could put a notion in his head:
'Why do they make good neighbours? Isn't it
Where there are cows? But here there are no cows.
Before I built a wall I'd ask to know
What I was walling in or walling out,
And to whom I was like to give offence.
Something there is that doesn't love a wall,
That wants it down.' I could say 'Elves' to him,
But it's not elves exactly, and I'd rather
He said it for himself. I see him there
Bringing a stone grasped firmly by the top

In each hand, like an old-stone savage armed.
He moves in darkness as it seems to me,
Not of woods only and the shade of trees.
He will not go behind his father's saying,
And he likes having thought of it so well
He says again, 'Good fences make good neighbours.'

Robert Frost

Hide and Seek

Call out. Call loud: 'I'm ready! Come and find me!'
The sacks in the toolshed smell like the seaside.
They'll never find you in this salty dark,
But be careful that your feet aren't sticking out.
Wiser not to risk another shout.
The floor is cold. They'll probably be searching
The bushes near the swing. Whatever happens
You mustn't sneeze when they come prowling in.
And here they are, whispering at the door;
You've never heard them sound so hushed before.
Don't breathe. Don't move. Stay dumb. Hide in your blindness.
They're moving closer, someone stumbles, mutters;
Their words and laughter scuffle, and they're gone.
But don't come out just yet; they'll try the lane
And then the greenhouse and back here again.
They must be thinking that you're very clever,
Getting more puzzled as they search all over.
It seems a long time since they went away.
Your legs are stiff, the cold bites through your coat;
The dark damp smell of sand moves in your throat.
It's time to let them know that you're the winner.
Push off the sacks. Uncurl and stretch. That's better!
Out of the shed and call to them: 'I've won!
Here I am! Come and own up I've caught you!'
The darkening garden watches. Nothing stirs.
The bushes hold their breath; the sun is gone.
Yes, here you are. But where are they who sought you?

Vernon Scannell

One Summer Evening ...

One summer evening (led by her) I found
A little boat tied to a willow tree
Within a rocky cove, its usual home.
Straight I unloosed her chain, and stepping in
Pushed from the shore. It was an act of stealth
And troubled pleasure, nor without the voice
Of mountain-echoes did my boat move on;
Leaving behind her still, on either side,
Small circles glittering idly in the moon,
Until they melted all into one track
Of sparkling light. But now, like one who rows,
Proud of his skill, to reach a chosen point
With an unswerving line, I fixed my view
Upon the summit of a craggy ridge,
The horizon's utmost boundary; far above
Was nothing but the stars and the grey sky.
She was an elfin pinnace; lustily
I dipped my oars into the silent lake,
And, as I rose upon the stroke, my boat
Went heaving through the water like a swan;
When, from behind that craggy steep till then
The horizon's bound, a huge peak, black and huge,
As if with voluntary power instinct,
Upreared its head. I struck and struck again,
And growing still in stature the grim shape
Towered up between me and the stars, and still,
For so it seemed, with purpose of its own
And measured motion like a living thing,
Strode after me. With trembling oars I turned,
And through the silent water stole my way
Back to the covert of the willow tree;
There in her mooring-place I left my bark, –
And through the meadows homeward went, in grave
And serious mood; but after I had seen
That spectacle, for many days, my brain
Worked with a dim and undetermined sense
Of unknown modes of being; o'er my thoughts
There hung a darkness, call it solitude

Or blank desertion. No familiar shapes
Remained, no pleasant images of trees,
Of sea or sky, no colours of green fields;
But huge and mighty forms, that do not live
Like living men, moved slowly through the mind
By day, and were a trouble to my dreams.

William Wordsworth (from 'The Prelude', Book 1)

The Fear

How often I turn round
To face the beast that bound by bound
Leaps on me from behind,
Only to see a bough that heaves
With sudden gust of wind
Or blackbird raking withered leaves.

A dog may find me out
Or badger toss a white-lined snout;
And one day as I softly trod
Looking for nothing stranger than
A fox or stoat I met a man
And even that seemed not too odd.

And yet in any place I go
I watch and listen as all creatures do
For what I cannot see or hear,
For something warns me everywhere
That even in my land of birth
I trespass on the earth.

Andrew Young

Desert Places

Snow falling and night falling fast, oh, fast
In a field I looked into going past,
And the ground almost covered smooth in snow,
But a few weeds and stubble showing last.

The woods around it have it – it is theirs.
All animals are smothered in their lairs.
I am too absent-minded to count;
The loneliness includes me unawares.

And lonely as it is that loneliness
Will be more lonely ere it will be less –
A blanker whiteness of benighted snow
With no expression, nothing to express.

They cannot scare me with their empty spaces
Between stars – on stars where no human race is.
I have it in me so much nearer home
To scare myself with my own desert places.

Robert Frost

Written in Northampton County Asylum

I am! yet what I am who cares, or knows?
　　My friends forsake me like a memory lost.
I am the self-consumer of my woes;
　　They rise and vanish, an oblivious host,
Shadows of life, whose very soul is lost.
And yet I am – I live – though I am tossed

Into the nothingness of scorn and noise,
　　Into the living sea of waking dream,
Where there is neither sense of life, nor joys,
　　But the huge shipwreck of my own esteem
And all that's dear. Even those I loved the best
Are strange – nay, they are stranger than the rest.

I long for scenes where man has never trod –
　　For scenes where woman never smiled or wept –
There to abide with my Creator, God,
　　And sleep as I in childhood sweetly slept,
Full of high thoughts, unborn. So let me lie, –
The grass below; above, the vaulted sky.

John Clare

Not Waving but Drowning

Nobody heard him, the dead man,
But still he lay moaning:
I was much further out than you thought
And not waving but drowning.

Poor chap, he always loved larking
And now he's dead
It must have been too cold for him his heart gave way,
They said.

Oh, no no no, it was too cold always
(Still the dead one lay moaning)
I was much too far out all my life
And not waving but drowning.

Stevie Smith

Richard Cory

Whenever Richard Cory went down town,
We people on the pavement looked at him;
He was a gentleman from sole to crown,
Clean favored, and imperially slim.

And he was always quietly arrayed,
And he was always human when he talked;
But still he fluttered pulses when he said,
'Good morning,' and he glittered when he walked.

And he was rich – yes, richer than a king –
And admirably schooled in every grace:
In fine, we thought he was everything
To make us wish that we were in his place.

So on we worked, and waited for the light,
And went without the meat, and cursed the bread;
And Richard Cory, one calm summer night,
Went home and put a bullet through his head.

Edwin Arlington Robinson

Old

I'm afraid of needles,
I'm tired of rubber sheets and tubes.
I'm tired of faces that I don't know
and now I think that death is starting.
Death starts like a dream,
full of objects and my sister's laughter.
We are young and we are walking
and picking wild blueberries
all the way to Damariscotta.
Oh Susan, she cried,
you've stained your new waist.
Sweet taste –
my mouth so full
and the sweet blue running out
all the way to Damariscotta.
What are you doing? Leave me alone!
Can't you see I'm dreaming?
In a dream you are never eighty.

Anne Sexton

The Astigmatic

At seven the sun that lit my world blew out
Leaving me only mist. Through which I probed
My way to school, guessed wildly at the sums
Whose marks on the board I couldn't even see.

They wanted to send me away to a special school.
I refused, and coped as best I could with half
The light lost in the mist, screwing my tears
Into my work, my gritted teeth, my writing –

Which crawled along and writhed. Think thoughts at will,
None of it comes across. Even now friends ask
'How do you read that scrawl?' The fact is, I don't;
Nobody could. I guess. But how would you

Like my world where parallels actually join,
Perspectives vary at sight? Once in a pub
I walked towards a sign marked gents over
A grating and crashed through the floor –

Well, it looked all right to me. Those steep stairs
People told me of later flattened to lines
In my half-world. The rest imagination
Supplied: when you've half a line you extend it.

The lenses drag their framework down my nose.
I still can't look strangers in the face,
Wilting behind a wall of glass at them.
It makes me look shifty at interviews.

I wake up with a headache, chew all day
Aspirins, go to bed dispirited,
Still with a dull pain somewhere in my skull,
And sleep. Then, in my dreams, the sun comes out.

Philip Hobsbaum

A Solitude

A blind man. I can stare at him
ashamed, shameless. Or does he know it?
No, he is in a great solitude.

O, strange joy,
to gaze my fill at a stranger's face.
No, my thirst is greater than before.

In his world he is speaking
almost aloud. His lips move.
Anxiety plays about them. And now joy

of some sort trembles into a smile.
A breeze I can't feel
crosses that face as if it crossed water.

The train moves uptown, pulls in and
pulls out of the local stops. Within its loud
jarring movement a quiet,

the quiet of people not speaking,
some of them eyeing the blind man,
only a moment though, not thirsty like me,

and within that quiet his
different quiet, not quiet at all, a tumult
of images, but what are his images,

he is blind? He doesn't care
that he looks strange, showing
his thoughts on his face like designs of light

flickering on water, for he doesn't know
what look is.
I see he has never seen.

And now he rises, he stands at the door ready,
knowing his station is next. Was he counting?
No, that was not his need.

When he gets out I get out.
'Can I help you towards the exit?'
'Oh, alright.' An indifference.

But instantly, even as he speaks,
even as I hear indifference, his hand
goes out, waiting for me to take it,

and now we hold hands like children.
His hand is warm and not sweaty,
the grip firm, it feels good.

And when we have passed through the turnstile,
he going first, his hand at once
waits for mine again.

'Here are the steps. And now we turn
to the right. More stairs now.' We go
up into sunlight. He feels that,

the soft air. 'A nice day,
isn't it?' says the blind man. Solitude
walks with me, walks

beside me, he is not with me, he continues
his thoughts alone. But his hand and mine
know one another,

it's as if my hand were gone forth
on its own journey. I see him
across the street, the blind man,

and now he says he can find his way. He knows
where he is going, it is nowhere, it is filled
with presences. He says, **I am.**

Denise Levertov

Fairy Tale

He built himself a house,
>his foundations,
>his stones,
>his walls,
>his roof overhead,
>his chimney and smoke,
>his view from the window.

He made himself a garden,
>his fence,
>his thyme,
>his earthworm,
>his evening dew.

He cut out his bit of sky above.

And he wrapped the garden in the sky
and the house in the garden
and packed the lot in a handkerchief

and went off
lone as an arctic fox
through the cold
unending
rain
into the world.

Miroslav Holub

The Lake Isle of Innisfree

I will arise and go now, and go to Innisfree,
And a small cabin build there, of clay and wattles made:
Nine bean-rows will I have there, a hive for the honey-bee,
And live alone in the bee-loud glade.

And I shall have some peace there, for peace comes dropping slow,
Dropping from the veils of the morning to where the cricket sings;
There midnight's all a glimmer, and noon a purple glow,
And evening full of the linnet's wings.

I will arise and go now, for always night and day
I hear lake water lapping with low sounds by the shore;
While I stand on the roadway, or on the pavements grey,
I hear it in the deep heart's core.

W B Yeats

Poems of Solitary Delights

What a delight it is
When on the bamboo matting
In my grass-thatched hut,
All on my own,
I make myself at ease.

What a delight it is
When, borrowing
Rare writings from a friend,
I open out
The first sheet.

What a delight it is
When, spreading paper,
I take my brush
And find my hand
Better than I thought.

What a delight it is
When, after a hundred days
Of racking my brains,
That verse that wouldn't come
Suddenly turns out well.

What a delight it is
When, of a morning,
I get up and go out
To find in full bloom a flower
That yesterday was not there.

What a delight it is
When, skimming through the pages
Of a book, I discover
A man written of there
Who is just like me.

What a delight it is
When everyone admits
It's a very difficult book,
And I understand it
With no trouble at all.

What a delight it is
When I blow away the ash,
To watch the crimson
Of the glowing fire
And hear the water boil.

What a delight it is
When a guest you cannot stand
Arrives, then says to you
'I'm afraid I can't stay long,'
And soon goes home.

What a delight it is
When I find a good brush,
Steep it hard in water,
Lick it on my tongue
And give it its first try.

Tachibana Akemi

The Hermit

I dwell apart
From the world of men.

I lift my eyes
To the mighty hills,
And sit in silent reverie
By rushing streams.
My songs
Are the whisperings of the winds
And the soft murmurs
Of falling rain.

Blossoms open
And flutter to earth again.
Men come
And men go;
Year follows year,
And life goes on.

Hsü Pên

If You Came

If you came to my secret glade,
    Weary with heat,
I would set you down in the shade,
    I would wash your feet.

If you came in the winter sad,
    Wanting for bread,
I would give you the last that I had,
    I would give you my bed.

But the place is hidden apart
    Like a nest by a brook,
And I will not show you my heart
    By a word, by a look.

The place is hidden apart
    Like the nest of a bird:
And I will not show you my heart
    By a look, by a word.

Ruth Pitter

The Soul Selects her own Society

The Soul selects her own Society –
Then – shuts the Door –
To her divine Majority –
Present no more –

Unmoved – she notes the Chariots – pausing –
At her low Gate –
Unmoved – an Emperor be kneeling
Upon her Mat –

I've known her – from an ample nation –
Choose One –
Then – close the Valves of her attention –
Like Stone –

Emily Dickinson

CONNECTIONS . . .

A Poison Tree

I was angry with my friend:
I told my wrath, my wrath did end.
I was angry with my foe:
I told it not, my wrath did grow.

And I water'd it in fears,
Night and morning with my tears;
And I sunned it with smiles,
And with soft deceitful wiles.

And it grew both day and night,
Till it bore an apple bright;
And my foe beheld it shine,
And he knew that it was mine,

And into my garden stole
When the night had veil'd the pole:
In the morning glad I see
My foe outstretch'd beneath the tree.

William Blake

The Angry Man

The other day I chanced to meet
An angry man upon the street –
A man of wrath, a man of war,
A man who truculently bore
Over his shoulder, like a lance,
A banner labeled 'Tolerance'.

And when I asked him why he strode
Thus scowling down the human road,
Scowling, he answered, 'I am he
Who champions total liberty –
Intolerance being, ma'am, a state
No tolerant man can tolerate.

'When I meet rogues,' he cried, 'who choose
To cherish oppositional views,
Lady, like this, and in this manner,
I lay about them with my banner
Till they cry mercy, ma'am.' His blows
Rained proudly on prospective foes.

Fearful, I turned and left him there
Still muttering, as he thrashed the air,
'Let the Intolerant beware!'

Phyllis McGinley

Africa's Plea

I am not you –
but you will not
give me a chance,
will not let me be *me*.

'If I were you' –
but you know
I am not you,
yet you will not
let me be *me*.

You meddle, interfere
in my affairs
as if they were yours
and you were me.

You are unfair, unwise,
foolish to think
that I can be you,
talk, act
and think like you.

God made me *me*.
He made you *you*.
For God's sake
Let me be *me*.

Roland Tombekai Dempster

The Hunched

They will not leave me, the lives of other people,
I wear them near my eyes like spectacles.
The sullen magnates, hunched into chins and overcoats
In the back seats of their large cars;
The scholars, so conscientious, as if to escape
The things too real, the names too easily read,
Preferring language stuffed with difficulties;
And the children, furtive with their own parts;
The lonely glutton in the sunlit corner
Of an empty Chinese restaurant;
The coughing woman, leaning on a wall,
Her wedding ring finger in her son's cold hand,
In her back the invisible arch of death.
What makes them laugh, who lives with them?
I stooped to lace a shoe, and they all came back,
Dull, mysterious people without names or faces,
Whose lives I guess about, whose dangers tease,
And not one of them has anything at all to do with me.

Douglas Dunn

My Parents Kept Me from Children who were Rough

My parents kept me from children who were rough
Who threw words like stones and who wore torn clothes.
Their thighs showed through rags. They ran in the street
And climbed cliffs and stripped by the country streams.

I feared more than tigers their muscles like iron
Their jerking hands and their knees tight on my arms.
I feared the salt coarse pointing of those boys
Who copied my lisp behind me on the road.

They were lithe, they sprang out behind hedges
Like dogs to bark at my world. They threw mud
While I looked the other way, pretending to smile.
I longed to forgive them, but they never smiled.

Stephen Spender

Parable

Two neighbours, who were rather dense,
Considered that their mutual fence
Were more symbolic of their peace
(Which they maintained should never cease)
If each about his home and garden
Set up a more substantial warden.
Quickly they cleared away the fence
To build a wall at great expense;
And soon their little plots of ground
Were barricaded all around:
Yet still they added stone to stone,
As if they never would be done,
For when one neighbour seemed to tire
The other shouted: *Higher! Higher!*
Thus day by day, in their unease,
They built the battlements of peace
Whose shadows, like a gathering blot,
Darkened on each neglected plot,
Until the ground, so overcast,
Became a rank and weedy waste.

Now in obsession, they uprear;
Jealous, and proud, and full of fear:
And, lest they halt for lack of stone,
They pull their dwelling-houses down.
At last, by their insane excess,
Their ramparts guard a wilderness;
And hate, arousing out of shame,
Flares up into a wondrous flame:
They curse; they strike; they break the wall
Which buries them beneath its fall.

William Soutar

The Fog

I saw the fog grow thick,
   Which soon made blind my ken;
It made tall men of boys,
   And giants of tall men.

It clutched my throat, I coughed;
   Nothing was in my head
Except two heavy eyes
   Like balls of burning lead.

And when it grew so black
   That I could know no place,
I lost all judgement then,
   Of distance and of space.

The street lamps, and the lights
   Upon the halted cars,
Could either be on earth
   Or be the heavenly stars.

A man passed by me close,
   I asked my way, he said,
'Come, follow me, my friend' –
   I followed where he led.

He rapped the stones in front,
   'Trust me,' he said, 'and come';
I followed like a child –
   A blind man led me home.

W H Davies

Shepherdess (A Love Poem)

All day my sheep have mingled with yours. They strayed
Into your valley seeking a change of ground.
Held and bemused with what they and I had found,
Pastures and wonders, heedlessly I delayed.

Now it is late. The tracks leading home are steep,
The stars and landmarks in your country are strange.
How can I take my sheep back over the range?
Shepherdess, show me now where I may sleep.

Norman Cameron

Song

O wert thou in the storm
   How I would shield thee:
To keep thee dry and warm,
   A camp I would build thee.

Though the clouds pour'd again,
   Not a drop should harm thee,
The music of wind, and rain,
   Rather should charm thee.

O wert thou in the storm,
   A shed I would build thee;
To keep thee dry and warm, –
   How I would shield thee.

The rain should not wet thee,
   Nor thunder clap harm thee.
By thy side I would sit me, –
   To comfort, and warm thee.

I would sit by thy side, love,
   While the dread storm was over; –
And the wings of an angel
   My charmer would cover.

John Clare

Meeting at Night

The grey sea and the long black land;
And the yellow half-moon large and low;
And the startled little waves that leap
In fiery ringlets from their sleep,
As I gain the cove with pushing prow,
And quench its speed i' the slushy sand.

Then a mile of warm sea-scented beach;
Three fields to cross till a farm appears;
A tap at the pane, the quick sharp scratch
And blue spurt of a lighted match,
And a voice less loud, through its joys and fears,
Than the two hearts beating each to each!

Robert Browning

Come Away, My Love

Come away, my love, from streets
Where unkind eyes divide,
And shop windows reflect our difference.
In the shelter of my faithful room, rest.

There, safe from opinions, being behind
Myself, I can see only you;
And in my dark eyes your grey
Will dissolve.

    The candlelight throws
Two dark shadows on the wall
Which merge into one as I close beside you.

When at last the lights are out,
And I feel your hand in mine,
Two human breaths join in one,
And the piano weaves
Its unchallenged harmony.

Joseph Kariuki

Home

Home is the place where the diseased world dies at the door,
where the floor and carpets are worn by familiar feet,
where you can close your eyes and nobody says you are blind.

Home is where you don't have to be polite and sing
      cane-sweet song to coat bitterness,
where familiarity accepts you in its security,
where you know that love still breathes somewhere,
where your wife and children keep the other half of you.

When the rain broadcasts the glass face of the fields
      and moves the tidemark of the canals,
when you do not know where to go,
home is where they never say 'no'.

The small cottage that sits cosily under the palms,
the atap, brown with time and age hangs to the field,
the complaining hinges and wet stairs,
home is you
and where you hope to die.

Mohammad Haji Salleh

An Old Jamaican Woman Thinks About the Hereafter

What would I do forever in a big place, who
have lived all my life in a small island?
The same parish holds the cottage I was born in, all
my family, and the cool churchyard.
                              I have looked
up at the stars from my front verandah and have been afraid
of their pathless distances. I have never flown
in the loud aircraft nor have I seen palaces,
so I would prefer not to be taken up high nor
rewarded with a large mansion.
                              I would like
to remain half drowsing through an evening light
watching bamboo trees sway and ruffle for a valley-wind,
to remember old times but not to live them again;
occasionally to have a good meal with no milk
nor honey for I don't like them, and now and then to walk
by the grey sea-beach with two old dogs and watch
men bring up their boats from the water.
                              For all this,
for my hope of heaven, I am willing to forgive my debtors
and to love my neighbour ...
                              although the wretch throws stones
at my white rooster and makes too much noise in her damn backyard.

A L Hendriks

People

Some people talk and talk
and never say a thing.
Some people look at you
and birds begin to sing.

Some people laugh and laugh
and yet you want to cry.
Some people touch your hand
and music fills the sky.

Charlotte Zolotow

Friends

I fear it's very wrong of me
And yet I must admit,
When someone offers friendship
I want the *whole* of it.
I don't want everybody else
To share my friends with me.
At least, I want *one* special one,
Who, indisputably,

Likes me much more than all the rest,
Who's always on my side,
Who never cares what others say,
Who lets me come and hide
Within his shadow, in his house –
It doesn't matter where
Who lets me simply be myself,
Who's always, *always* there.

Elizabeth Jennings

Who is There? Me

Who is there? Me.
Me who? I am me. You are you.
You take my pronoun
And we are us.

Kenneth Rexroth (trans. of Marichiko poem)

...AND SEPARATIONS...

In Former Days

In former days we'd both agree
That you were me, and I was you.
What has now happened to us two,
That you are you, and I am me?

Bhartrhari

Walking Away

It is eighteen years ago, almost to the day –
A sunny day with the leaves just turning,
The touch-lines new-ruled – since I watched you play
Your first game of football, then, like a satellite
Wrenched from its orbit, go drifting away

Behind a scatter of boys. I can see
You walking away from me towards the school
With the pathos of a half-fledged thing set free
Into a wilderness, the gait of one
Who finds no path where the path should be.

That hesitant figure, eddying away
Like a winged seed loosened from its parent stem,
Has something I never quite grasp to convey
About nature's give-and-take – the small, the scorching
Ordeals which fire one's irresolute clay.

I have had worse partings, but none that so
Gnaws at my mind still. Perhaps it is roughly
Saying what God alone could perfectly show –
How selfhood begins with a walking away,
And love is proved in the letting go.

Cecil Day Lewis

Hesitant

He sees beyond her face another face.
It is the one he wants.
He stares at it in amazement;
There is nothing anywhere quite like it.
There is nothing else that's wanted.

She sees beyond his face another face.
It stares at her in amazement.
She stares back, equally amazed.
Just why, she can't quite answer.
She simply wants it.

These faces have been waiting now
A long time to be introduced.
If only the faces in front
Would do something about it.

Brian Patten

Will You Come?

Will you come?
Will you come
Will you ride
So late
At my side?
O, will you come?

Will you come?
Will you come
If the night
Has a moon,
Full and bright?
O, will you come?

Would you come?
Would you come
If the noon
Gave light,
Not the moon?
Beautiful, would you come?

Would you have come?
Would you have come
Without scorning,
Had it been
Still morning?
Beloved, would you have come?

If you come
Haste and come.
Owls have cried;
It grows dark
To ride,
Beloved, beautiful, come.

Edward Thomas

Since There's No Help

Since there's no help, come let us kiss and part –
Nay, I have done; you get no more of me;
And I am glad, yea, glad with all my heart,
That thus so cleanly I myself can free.
Shake hands forever; cancel all our vows;
And when we meet at any time again,
Be it not seen in either of our brows
That we one jot of former love retain.

Now at the last gasp of Love's latest breath
When, his pulse failing, Passion speechless lies,
When Faith is kneeling by his bed of death
And Innocence is closing up his eyes,
   – Now, if thou would'st, when all have given him over,
   From death to life thou might'st him yet recover.

Michael Drayton

Song

Sweetest love, I do not go
  For weariness of thee,
Nor in hope the world can show
  A fitter love for me;
    But since that I
Must die at last, 'tis best
To use myself in jest
  Thus by fain'd deaths to die.

Yesternight the sun went hence,
  And yet is here today,
He hath no desire nor sense,
  Nor half so short a way:
    Then fear not me,
But believe that I shall make
Speedier journeys, since I take
  More wings and spurs than he.

O how feeble is man's power,
  That if good fortune fall,
Cannot add another hour,
  Nor a lost hour recall!
    But come bad chance,
And we join to it our strength,
And we teach it art and length,
  Itself o'er us to advance.

When thou sigh'st, thou sigh'st not wind,
  But sigh'st my soul away,
When thou weep'st, unkindly kind,
  My life's blood doth decay.
    It cannot be
That thou lov'st me, as thou say'st,
If in thine my life thou waste,
  Thou art the best of me.

Let not thy divining heart
  Forethink me any ill,
Destiny may take thy part,
  And may thy fears fulfil;
    But think that we
Are but turn'd aside to sleep;
They who one another keep
    Alive, ne'er parted be.

John Donne

The River-Merchant's Wife: A Letter

While my hair was still cut straight across my forehead
I played about the front gate, pulling flowers.
You came by on bamboo stilts, playing horse,
You walked about my seat, playing with blue plums.
And we went on living in the village of Chōkan:
Two small people, without dislike or suspicion.

At fourteen I married My Lord you.
I never laughed, being bashful.
Lowering my head, I looked at the wall.
Called to, a thousand times, I never looked back.

At fifteen I stopped scowling,
I desired my dust to be mingled with yours
Forever and forever and forever.
Why should I climb the lookout?

At sixteen you departed,
You went into far Ku-tō-en, by the river of swirling eddies,
And you have been gone five months.
The monkeys make sorrowful noise overhead.

You dragged your feet when you went out.
By the gate now, the moss is grown, the different mosses,
Too deep to clear them away!
The leaves fall early this autumn, in wind.
The paired butterflies are already yellow with August
Over the grass in the West garden;
They hurt me. I grow older.
If you are coming down through the narrows of the river Kiang,
Please let me know beforehand,
And I will come out to meet you
    As far as Chō-fū-Sa.

By Rihaku (Li T'ai Po), 8th century A.D.

Ezra Pound

116

The Bustle in a House

The Bustle in a House
The Morning after Death
Is solemnest of industries
Enacted upon earth –

The Sweeping up the Heart,
And putting Love away
We shall not want to use again
Until Eternity.

Emily Dickinson

When I am Dead

When I am dead
Cry for me a little
Think of me sometimes
But not too much.
Think of me now and again
As I was in life
At some moments it's pleasant to recall
But not for long.
Leave me in peace
And I shall leave you in peace
And while you live
Let your thoughts be with the living.

Anon. (trad. Indian)

Index of Poets

The Artists

The illustrations are by

Alan Baker: pp 29, 33, 65, 68, 71
Prue Berthon: pp 47, 49, 53, 109, 111, 115
Robert Geary: pp 37, 43, 57, 61
Sheila Ratcliffe: pp 11, 16, 77, 81, 83, 86, 91
Barry Wilkinson: pp 21, 25, 27, 95, 99, 100, 105

Index of Titles and First Lines

(titles are in bold print, first lines in italics)

ACKNOWLEDGEMENTS

We are grateful for permission to include the following copyright poems in this anthology:

Akemi Tachibana: 'Poems of Solitary Delights', from *The Penguin Book of Japanese Verse* trans. Geoffrey Bownas and Anthony Thwaite (Penguin Books, 1964), trans. copyright © Geoffrey Bownas and Anthony Thwaite, 1964, pp. 142–3. Reprinted by permission of Penguin Books Ltd.

Conrad Aiken: 'Crickets' from 'Time in the Rock', part XII, pp. 675–6, from *Collected Poems* (OUP New York).

Anon: 'But No One Cares' from *Children As Poets*, ed. Denys Thompson. Reprinted by permission of Mrs E. Thompson.

Martin Armstrong: 'Mrs Reece Laughs' from *Collected Poems* (Martin Secker & Warburg Ltd). Reprinted by permission of Peters Fraser & Dunlop Group Ltd.

W.H. Auden: 'The Unknown Citizen' from *Collected Poems*, ed. Edward Mendelson. Copyright 1940 and renewed 1968 by W.H. Auden. Reprinted by permission of Random House Inc., and Faber & Faber Ltd.

Bhartrhari: 'In Former Days', from *Poems from the Sanskrit* trans. John Brough (Penguin Books, 1968), copyright © John Brough, 1968, p. 57. Reprinted by permission of Penguin Books Ltd.

Morris Bishop: 'Ambition' from *The Best of Bishop; Light Verse from The New Yorker and Elsewhere* (Cornell). Copyright 1950, © 1978 Alison Kingsbury Bishop. Originally in The New Yorker. Used by permission.

Anne Bloch: 'Dreams'.*

Norman Cameron: 'Shepherdess' from *Collected Poems*. Reprinted by permission of Chatto & Windus on behalf of the author.

Charles Causley: 'Healing a Lunatic Boy' from *Union Street*; 'Timothy Winters' from *Collected Poems* and 'Green Man, Blue Man' from *Figgie Hobbin*. Reprinted by permission of David Higham Associates Ltd.

Peter Clarke: 'Young Shepherd Bathing His Feet' from *Poems From Black Africa*, ed. Langston Hughes.*

Frances Cornford: 'Childhood' from *Collected Poems*. Reprinted by permission of Century Hutchinson Ltd.

e. e. cummings: 'may my heart always be open to little' from *Complete Poems 1913–1962*. Copyright © 1923, 1925, 1931, 1935, 1938, 1939, 1940, 1944, 1945, 1946, 1947, 1948, 1949, 1950, 1951, 1952, 1953, 1954, 1955, 1956, 1957, 1958, 1959, 1960, 1961, 1962 by the Trustees for the E E Cummings Trust. Copyright © 1961, 1963, 1968 by Marion Morehouse Cummings. Reprinted by permission of Grafton Books, a division of the Collins Publishing Group and Liveright Publishing Corp. Inc.

Ruth Dallas: 'Grandmother and Child' from *Collected Poems*, University of Otago Press, 1987. Reprinted by permission of the author.

Elizabeth Daryush: 'Anger lay by me all night long' from *Collected Poems*. Reprinted by permission of Carcanet Press Ltd.

W.H. Davies: 'The Fog', copyright © 1963 by Jonathan Cape Ltd., from *The Complete Poems of W.H. Davies*. Reprinted by permission of Jonathan Cape Ltd. on behalf of the Executors of the W.H. Davies Estate, and Wesleyan University Press.

Roland Tombekai Dempster: 'Africa's Plea' from *Poems From Black Africa*, ed. Langston Hughes.*

Emily Dickinson: 'Nobody', 'To Make a Prairie', 'The Soul Selects her own Society' and 'The Bustle in the House'. Reprinted by permission of the publishers and the Trustees of Amherst College from *The Poems of Emily Dickinson*, ed. Thomas H. Johnson, Cambridge, Mass.: The Belknap Press of Harvard University Press, Copyright 1951, © 1955, 1979, 1983 by The President and Fellows of Harvard College.

Olive Dove: 'Write a Poem'. Reprinted by permission of the author.

Douglas Dunn: 'The Hunched' from *The Happier Life*. Reprinted by permission of Faber & Faber Ltd.

Sheikha A El-Miskery: 'Just a Word' from D. Cook & D. Rubadiri (eds.), *Poems from East Africa* (Heinemann Educational Books Ltd.).

Andrew Young: 'The Fear' from *Collected Poems*. Reprinted by permission of Martin Secker & Warburg Ltd.

Mei Yüan: 'Expression of Feelings, VII' from *The Penguin Book of Chinese Verse*, trans. Robert Kotewall and Norman L. Smith (Penguin Books, 1962), trans. copyright © N.L. Smith and R.H. Kotewall, 1962, p. 69. Reprinted by permission of Penguin Books Ltd.

Charlotte Zolotow: 'People' from *All That Sunlight*. Text copyright © 1967 by Charlotte Zolotow. Reprinted by permission of Harper & Row, Publishers, Inc.

Public Domain
Edwin Arlington Robinson: 'Miniver Cheevy' from *The Town Down the River* (New York: Scribner's 1910). 'Richard Cory' from *The Children of the Night* (New York: Scribner's, 1897).

Entries marked * indicate where we have been unable to trace or contact copyright holder prior to publication. If contacted, the publisher will be pleased to rectify any errors or omissions at the earliest opportunity.